FORT PULASKI

NATIONAL MONUMENT · *Georgia*

by
Ralston B. Lattimore

NATIONAL PARK SERVICE HISTORICAL HANDBOOK SERIES No. 18
Washington, D. C., 1954
(Reprint 1961)

The National Park System, of which Fort Pulaski National Monument is a unit, is dedicated to conserving the scenic, scientific, and historic heritage of the United States for the benefit and inspiration of its people.

Contents

FROM THE DAWN OF HISTORY *to the present, men have labored unceasingly to surround their homes with impregnable fortifications while at the same time they have tried to discover more powerful weapons to smash through the defenses of other men. The Romans and the Chinese had their great walls; the feudal lords of the Middle Ages had their moated castles; and to modern times belong the Maginot and the Siegfried Lines and the atom bombs. In these great efforts, and countless others like them, man has confidently sought permanent security. But no man or nation has yet devised a refuge safe against new weapons and new tactics of a determined enemy. The age-old struggle between offense and defense is the principal story of Fort Pulaski.*

Cockspur Island, 1733–1829

After gathering its waters from the high valleys and slopes of the Appalachian Mountains, the Savannah River follows a course southeastward 300 miles to the sea and forms a natural boundary between South Carolina and Georgia. Plunging swiftly through narrow gorges or drowsing through cypress swamps, this brown-red river moves onward past pine-crested hills and smothered plains. Twelve miles from the sea it leaves the firm land to sweep in lazy coils across a vast and quivering marsh. Here the river splits into two channels divided by low grassy islets almost completely submerged twice daily by the rising of the tide. The easternmost of these islets, a mile long by less than half a mile wide, is known as Cockspur Island from the shape of its dangerous reef that juts out toward the open sound.

Within sight of the Atlantic Ocean, Cockspur guards the two entrances into the Savannah River, one of the Nation's great avenues of commerce. Despite the fact that very few of its hundred or more acres lie above the highwater mark, this island has played a significant

Sketch above: **Fort George, 1761,** From a drawing by De Brahm.
—— *The walls and moat of Fort Pulaski,* Photo by Franklin Dulany.

role in the economic development and military defense of coastal Georgia throughout the history of colony and state. The island was considered so important that one Royal Governor called it the "Key to Our Province," and 20 acres on the eastern point were permanently set aside by the Crown and later by the State as a site for harbor fortifications.

To the north and south of Cockspur lie the barrier islands of the Carolina and Georgia coasts. On these great islands, and on mainland plantations across the marshes, aristocratic planters with many slaves developed the culture of rice, indigo, and cotton and helped to lay the foundation of an agrarian economy in the South, a factor which was to play a leading role in the controversies which divided the Nation in the 19th century and led to civil war.

Past Cockspur Island, then called "The Peeper," in February 1733 sailed the pioneer band of English settlers under Gen. James Edward Oglethorpe. At Yamacraw Bluff, 20 miles up the river, they established Savannah, the small settlement which was the beginning of Georgia, the 13th American colony. To Cockspur Island, John Wesley, founder of Methodism, made a momentous visit 3 years later. Here, his journal records, he ". . . first set . . . foot on American ground." More important in the history of religion, Wesley, during this sojourn at Cockspur, engaged in serious theological discussions which seem to have implanted in his mind the basic idea of Methodism.

A few years later Colonial leaders, fearing an attack by their perennial enemies at Spanish St. Augustine, advocated the construction of a fort on Cockspur Island to protect the growing port of Savannah. As a result Fort George, a palisaded log blockhouse, was begun in 1761 under the supervision of His Majesty's Surveyor-General John Gerar William de Brahm. This pioneer fort on Cockspur Point provided a measure of defense for the Savannah harbor, but principally enforced quarantine and customs regulations, until the revolutionary activities of 1776 when it was dismantled and abandoned by the Patriots, who knew the fortification could not stand against a strong fleet.

Soon after Fort George was abandoned, two British warships, accompanied by a transport, arrived in Tybee Roads bent on securing fresh provisions and information regarding the uprising in Georgia. Under their formidable guns Cockspur Island served as a haven for Loyalists fleeing from Savannah. Among the refugees was the Royal Governor, Sir James Wright, who escaped to the island on the night of February 11, 1776. As he carried with him the great seal of the Province, Cockspur Island became briefly the capital of colonial Georgia. In March, the British ships boldly sailed up the river to Savannah where they engaged the Patriots in a brief clash of arms and made off with several ships laden with rice. With these events the story of Cockspur Island in the Revolution was virtually at an end. When the British returned in

John Wesley. Engraving by John Faber, Jr., from a portrait by John Michael Williams. Courtesy Mrs. Craig Barrow.

force to reoccupy Savannah in December 1778, the great fleet rendez-voused at the anchorage off Cockspur Point, but the island lay deserted and undisturbed.

After the United States was established as a nation, new defenses were needed to safeguard the young republic, and, in accord with President Washington's national defense policy, a second fort was built in 1794–95, on Cockspur Island. Named Fort Greene in honor of the Revolutionary hero, Gen. Nathanael Greene, who after the war made his home at Mulberry Grove Plantation near Savannah, this fortification consisted of a battery designed for six guns, and was constructed of timbers and earth enclosed behind pickets. There was also a guardhouse for the garrison.

The history of Fort Greene was brief and tragic. Nine years after the fort was built, it was totally destroyed and a part of the garrison was drowned in the great hurricane that swept Cockspur in September 1804. Huge sea waves raked the island from end to end until not a vestige of the fort remained. A quarter of a century was then to elapse before Cockspur Island was again to be selected as the site of a fortification to command the Savannah River.

3

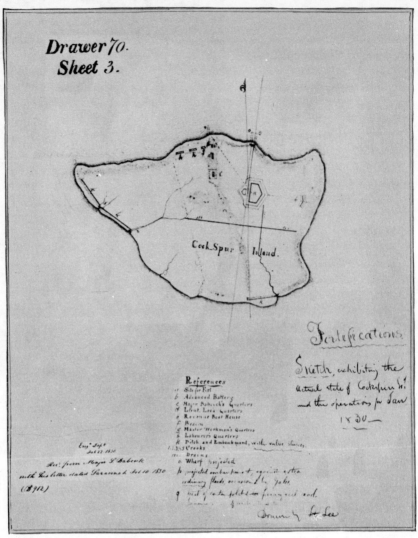

Cock Spur Island.

References
a Site for Fort
b Advanced Battery
c Major Babcock's Quarters
d Lieut. Lee's Quarters
e Revenue Boat House
f Beacon
g Master Workman's Quarters
h Labourers Quarters
k Ditch and Embankment, with value sluices.
l,1,2,3 Creeks
m Drains
o Wharf projected

Fortifications.

Sketch, exhibiting the actual state of Cockspur Id. and the operations for Jan 1830—

Eng.r Dep.t
July 22 1830
Rec.d from Major L. Babcock
with his letter dated Savannah Jul 10 1830
(8912)

Drawn by R. Lee

Sketch of Cockspur Island by Lt. Robert E. Lee, 1830.

The New Fort on Cockspur

The United States can be proud of her victories in the War of 1812, but there were also defeats. It was fortunate that while England was fighting on this side of the Atlantic, her principal forces were engaged in a death struggle with Napoleon on the continent of Europe. American defenses were deplorably weak. On thousands of miles of coastline there was scarcely a fort to oppose the enemy. British troops pillaged and burned the city of Washington and laid waste to many sections

4

along the Middle Atlantic States. This humiliating and tragic lesson soon aroused public opinion to demand strong measures for protection.

After the Treaty of Ghent in 1814, which terminated the war with Britain, President James Madison urged Congress to appropriate funds to complete all forts then under construction and to extend the system of fortifications in order that the United States might at all times be prepared to prevent or repel the danger of foreign invasion.

The task of developing entirely new and adequate fortifications along the far-flung Atlantic and Gulf coasts was one which required the direction of a military expert with special engineering abilities. The Government's search for a person peculiarly fitted for this position resulted in securing the services of the distinguished French fortification and military engineer, Gen. Simon Bernard, who was then seeking employment in the United States.

A graduate of the École Polytechnique in Paris, Bernard had served with distinction in many of the campaigns of Napoleon. He displayed such outstanding abilities in fortification and engineering tactics that he soon acquired an enviable reputation. In 1815, after the Battle of Waterloo, he came to the United States at the suggestion of Joseph Bonaparte, bearing high recommendations to government officials from Lafayette and Albert Gallatin. With the consent of Congress, which had authorized the employment of a "skillful assistant," President Madison commissioned Bernard in the Corps of Engineers with the rank of brigadier general by brevet. Early in December 1816, by direct order of the President, General Bernard, Col. William McRee, and Col. Joseph G. Totten formed a new "Board of Engineers," the duties of which were to devise a system of seacoast defense for the entire country.

President Monroe, who succeeded Madison, was even more energetic than his predecessor in promoting the construction of new defenses. During his administration fortification policies were established, surveys were completed, and funds were provided to start construction.

Diamondback terrapin. Sketch by Robert E. Lee, Cockspur Island, 1831. Courtesy F. B. Screven.

Cockspur Island was chosen as the site for a new fort in March 1821, when the river approaches to Savannah were surveyed by Capt. John Le Conte under the personal supervision of Bernard, but construction on Cockspur was not begun until 1829. Plans approved by Bernard in 1827 proved to be unsuitable and a revised plan was prepared in 1831. The fort, as originally designed, was a massive 2-story structure mounting 3 tiers of guns. The deep mud of Cockspur, however, offered no foundation for so great a weight. In revising the plans, it was necessary to reduce the height of the walls and to provide heavy wooden piles and grillage to support the brick masonry.

Maj. Samuel Babcock, of the Corps of Engineers, was placed in charge of construction in December 1828, and work got under way early in the following year. Difficulty was encountered almost immediately in establishing title to the island, ownership of which was divided between private interests and the State of Georgia. In colonial days, from 4 to 20 acres on Cockspur Point had been reserved by the Crown for public use, and after the Revolution title to the Crown land became vested in the State. The two earlier forts, George and Greene, had been erected within this special reserve. The western portion of Cockspur, embracing approximately 150 acres, was granted in 1759 by George II to Jonathan Bryan, Esq., from whom it passed, through several hands, to the heirs of Edward Telfair, Governor of Georgia. On March 15, 1830, the Telfair interests were purchased by the United States for $5,000, and 15 years later the State of Georgia ceded the public lands on Cockspur Point to the Federal Government.

Late in 1829, Robert E. Lee, newly graduated from the United States Military Academy at West Point, was appointed to duty under Babcock. It was his first military assignment. Young Lee had the title of "acting assistant commissary of subsistence," but, because of his superior officer's ill health, he actually ran the job for more than a year until Babcock was succeeded by Lt. Joseph K. F. Mansfield. Lee began the system of drainage and dikes for the island. He made numerous surveys and located the permanent site for the fort. To Mansfield, however, who served on Cockspur from 1831 to 1845, belongs chief credit for construction. His great engineering ability, combined with a passionate devotion to duty, enabled him to overcome almost insurmountable difficulties to complete the fort.

In 1833, the new fort was named Pulaski in honor of the Polish hero, Count Casimir Pulaski, who fought in the American Revolution and was mortally wounded at the Battle of Savannah on October 9, 1779. While rallying French and American forces in an attack on a strong British redoubt, Pulaski was struck in the thigh by a grape shot. He died 2 days later, and, according to tradition, was buried at sea near the mouth of the Savannah River.

Work progressed at Fort Pulaski more or less continuously from 1829 to 1847, the year in which construction was essentially completed. It was an enormous project. Bricks were bought in lots of from 1 to 7 million, and it is probable that as many as 25,000,000 were put into

Savannah, 1837. Tempera painting by F. Cerveau. Courtesy Georgia Historical Society.

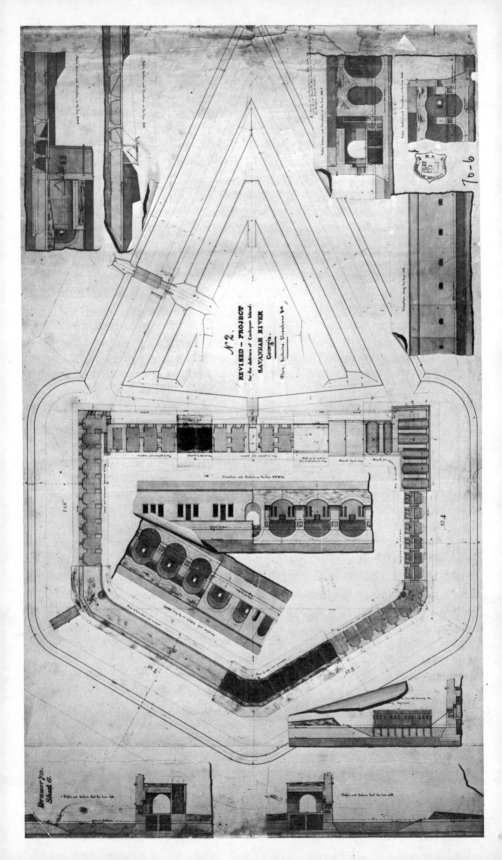

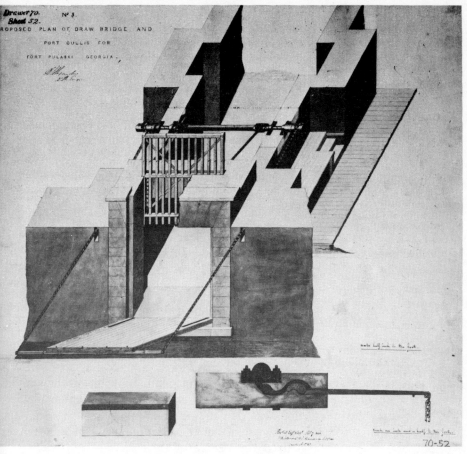

Fort Pulaski plan on opposite page and drawbridge plan above. Courtesy National Archives.

the structure. Lumber, lime, lead, iron, and many other supplies were bought in proportionately large quantities. The rose-brown bricks, of which the walls are largely built, were manufactured at the old Hermitage Plantation 2 miles west of Savannah. The much harder, rose-red bricks in the embrasures, arches, and the walls facing the parade ground were purchased in Baltimore, Md., and Alexandria, Va. The granite was quarried in New York State and the brown sandstone in the valley of the Connecticut River. Negro slaves, rented from the owners of neighboring rice plantations, performed many of the hard labor jobs, while skilled masons and carpenters were recruited not only in Savannah but were also brought down each fall from Northern States.

Throughout the long years of Mansfield's service on Cockspur Island there were many frustrating delays. There were summers in which all work had to stop because of the danger from malaria, yellow fever,

9

typhoid, and dysentery. There were periods when Congress failed to appropriate funds. At least once, Mansfield continued to build on credit—a bold expedient, which no Government servant today would dare to follow. There were also destructive hurricanes and bone-chilling winter gales. By the end of his tour of duty Mansfield was thoroughly discouraged, but through his determined perseverance he has left an enduring monument.

Nearly a million dollars had been spent on Fort Pulaski by the end of 1860, but in one respect it was not yet finished. Its armament was to include 146 guns, but only 20 guns had been mounted. Nor had the fort yet been garrisoned. At the end of 1860, its entire complement included a caretaker and an ordnance sergeant. For three decades, however, the project on Cockspur Island had served as a training ground for the Corps of Engineers, and with the exception of Major Babcock, who died in 1831, every engineer officer employed on the construction of the fort finally achieved the distinction of becoming a general in either the Confederate or the Union armies.

"Don't Tread on Me"

When Abraham Lincoln won the national presidential election on November 6, 1860, relations between North and South, already dangerously strained, reached the breaking point. Lincoln, candidate of the Republican Party, was supported also by a radical element in the North and West that was demanding the abolition of slavery. Reaction in the South to the result of the election was immediate. Southern secessionists stirred the people of their section with fiery speeches and sought to withdraw their States from the Union. Southern conservatives tried to find a way out of political chaos by compromise, but their task was hopeless. A whole generation had failed to discover a successful plan by which the two sections of the country could live at peace. The struggle had now gone beyond the bounds of a political campaign; two divergent cultures stood face to face on the threshold of war.

With remarkable clarity of vision Gov. Joseph E. Brown of Georgia began to put his State in a condition of defense many months in advance of hostilities. The State volunteer military forces were reorganized and strengthened, and many new volunteer companies were formed. On his recommendation the legislature appropriated a million dollars for State defense, authorized the acceptance of 10,000 troops, and provided for a convention on January 16, 1861, to determine the future course of Georgia.

Meanwhile, Governor Brown continued to rush preparations for defense. He obtained from the War Department sample sets of U. S.

Georgia troops on parade before the Pulaski Monument in Savannah. Frank Leslie's Illustrated Weekly, 1861.

Army infantry and cavalry equipment, which he proposed to manufacture in Georgia. The Secretary of War also described, on request, the type of rifled cannons and projectiles which the War Department had found superior. Orders for cannon and arms were placed in Northern States, and a bonus of $10,000 was offered by the State to anyone setting up a cannon factory in Georgia which could make 3 guns a week and could cast a 10-inch columbiad.

In the midst of these preparations came the announcement that South Carolina had seceded from the Union on December 20. The news of this action was received in Georgia with demonstrations of wild excitement. In Savannah, people wearing secession cockades made of palmetto leaves erected a platform in one of the principal squares on which they placed a large picture of a rattlesnake with the inscription, "Don't Tread on Me." On the evening of December 26, companies of militia and citizens marched with torch lights and transparencies through the streets of Savannah in honor of South Carolina, and houses all over the community were brilliantly illuminated.

Simultaneously an event was taking place in Charleston, S. C., that was to have an almost immediate effect on the course of action in Georgia, and, in fact, on the destiny of the entire South.

On that same evening, Maj. Robert Anderson, in command of the United States troops stationed in Charleston Harbor, moved his small garrison from an insecure position at Fort Moultrie on Sullivan's Island, to Fort Sumter, a strong fortification in the middle of the harbor. This unexpected move enraged not only the people of Charleston, but of all the slave-holding States. President James Buchanan, it was understood, had assured the Government of South Carolina that no change in the status of the United States forces at Charleston would be made until the difficulties between the State and Federal Governments had been settled. Major Anderson, however, fearing that an attack was imminent, evacuated Fort Moultrie with great secrecy, spiked the cannons and burned most of the gun carriages.

The news of the occupation of Fort Sumter, which reached Savannah by telegraph early Thursday morning, December 27, stunned the people, it is said, like "an electric shock." Groups of angry citizens gathered on the streets to discuss the news and to give vent to their feelings. "There is but one sentiment on the question," announced the Savannah *Republican,* "and that is of indignation and resistance . . . We might have been quieted by a milder course, but there are none of us so degraded as to submit to being whipped into submission."

Federal forces in possession of Fort Sumter had Charleston Harbor blocked. The same danger, it was argued at a meeting of civil and military leaders, threatened the Georgia seaport, for, if it was the policy of the United States to provoke a war, the Federal Government, in furtherance of that policy, would occupy and hold all forts commanding the harbors of the Southern States. For their own safety, therefore, the people of Savannah determined to seize Fort Pulaski before the Federal Government had time to send a garrison to defend it.

Military men in Savannah realized the gravity of taking so serious a step toward revolution as, no doubt, did thoughtful civilians, but the popular spirit of the mob had been stirred to the point of spontaneous action. On the night of December 31, the Savannah *Republican* received a copy of an ominous telegram to Alexander H. Stephens from United States Senator Robert Toombs, of Georgia. In this telegram Toombs warned the State of Georgia that a policy of coercion had been adopted by the Administration, that Joseph Holt, a bitter foe of the South, had been made Secretary of War, that the abolitionists were defiant, and that, in consequence, Fort Pulaski was in danger. The time had come for action.

Early next morning, Col. Alexander R. Lawton, in command of the 1st Volunteer Regiment of Georgia, telegraphed Governor Brown requesting him to come to Savannah at once. The Governor arrived

Gov. Joseph E. Brown, who ordered the seizure of Fort Pulaski. From Avery's *History of Georgia.*

Col. Alexander R. Lawton, who seized Fort Pulaski. Courtesy the late Mrs. A. R. Lawton, Sr.

about 9 p. m., and, after several meetings with leading citizens and military men, ordered the State militia to seize Fort Pulaski.

As there were no Federal troops garrisoned at Fort Pulaski, no difficulty was anticipated in seizing it, but the task of preparing an expedition in 24 hours for the purpose of occupying the stronghold was not a small matter. Arms, ammunition, and equipment had to be provided, commissary supplies purchased, and a steamboat for the transportation of men and baggage to Cockspur Island had to be secured. Detachments of 50 men each from the Savannah Volunteer Guards and the Oglethorpe Light Infantry and 34 men from the Chatham Artillery were selected to make the expedition. Each man was instructed to carry with him a knapsack containing a change of clothing, iron spoon, knife, fork, tin cup, clothesbrush, shoebrush, box of blacking, and a comb and brush.

Early next morning, January 3, 1861, the troops assembled in a pouring rain and marched through streets lined with cheering citizens to the wharf at the foot of West Broad Street, where they embarked on the U. S. Government sidewheel steamboat, *Ida,* for the journey down the river. In personal command was Colonel Lawton. This small expeditionary force is said to have carried enough baggage to have served a division later in the war. Every soldier had a trunk,

a cot, and a roll of bedding, while to every 3 or 4 men there was a huge mess chest large enough for the cooking outfit of a full regiment. Aboard also was the battery of the Chatham Artillery, which consisted of two 12-pounder howitzers and four 6-pounder field guns, all bronze.

At noon, the Savannah troops reached Cockspur Island and marched into Fort Pulaski with drums beating and colors flying. Colonel Lawton took formal possession of the fortification and the flag of Georgia was raised above the ramparts and saluted. No resistance was encountered. As the troops marched out on the parade ground of the fort, clouds which had obscured the sky for nearly a week broke away and the sun shone brightly. This was taken as a good omen. Georgia was now in possession of the strong fortification at the mouth of the Savannah River. The Governor's orders were to hold it against all persons and to abandon it only under new orders from him or under compulsion by an overpowering hostile force.

Under the Georgia Flag

Fort Pulaski was in no condition for defense on January 3 nor for many weeks thereafter. Had the Federal Government taken immediate and effective action, the incident on Cockspur Island might have ended quickly in complete fiasco. When Capt. Francis S. Bartow of the Oglethorpe Light Infantry took command of the post there was not a single serviceable gun in the fort. The moat was filled with mud and overgrown with marsh grass. Furthermore, the military experience of the members of his garrison had been limited to armory drill and dress parade.

During the first weeks after the seizure there was feverish activity to put the fort in condition required to withstand attack. Twenty 32-pounder naval guns, which had been mounted in 1840, were remounted in the casemates and on the ramparts. More than 100 ricefield slaves were engaged to dig the mud from the moat, and daily boat service was established between Savannah and Cockspur Island.

For a few days the garrison was in a state of great confusion. Baggage, which had preceded the troops, was hopelessly mixed up. Some squads with food had no pots to cook it in, while other squads with an abundance of pots and pans had no knives or forks with which to eat. Strict discipline, however, soon brought order out of chaos. All day the men were kept busy. They drilled in the manual of arms and learned to handle artillery. They sorted and redistributed equipment, filled mattress covers with hay, made cartridge bags, and stowed their ammunition in the magazines. Spirits were high and the men worked with a will.

As additional guns were secured they were mounted and others were ordered from the Tredegar Iron Works in Richmond. A telegraph line was erected between Savannah and Cockspur Island.

The Republican Blues of Savannah. Harper's Weekly, 1860.

Earthworks were constructed and manned on Hilton Head Island, in South Carolina, Tybee Island, and other islands southward along the Georgia coast. Fort Jackson, 5 miles below Savannah, was placed in order and work was begun on an interior line of defenses from Red Bluff on the north bank of the Savannah River delta to Genesis Point on the south bank of the Great Ogeechee.

The land defenses were supplemented by a small fleet of river boats on which guns had been mounted. This motley collection of side-wheelers, known as the Georgia Navy, was under the command of Commodore Josiah Tattnall, famous old naval officer, who years before had brought United States ships to the rescue of the British in China waters with the battle cry "Blood is thicker than water."

In the late spring of 1861, the defenses of Savannah were not yet perfect but they were rapidly gaining in strength. In company with Commodore Tattnall and General Lawton, William Howard Russell, correspondent of the *London Times,* inspected these defenses on May 1.

At Cockspur Island, Russell found a guard on duty at the landing, "tall, stout young fellows in various uniforms or in rude mufti, in which the Garibaldian red shirt and felt slouched hats predominated. They were armed with smoothbore muskets (date 1851), quite new; and their bayonets, barrels and locks were quite bright and clean. The officer on duty was dressed in blue frock coat with brass buttons emblazoned with the arms of the State, a red silk sash, and glazed kepi, and straw colored gauntlets."

Russell was impressed by the strength and solidity of the fort and by the preparations being made for its defense. He found its garrison of 650 men hard at work. Tents were pitched in the demilune and on the terreplein, and the parade ground presented a scene of life and animation. Men were building sandbag traverses to guard the magazine doors. Other were rolling away stores and casks of ammunition and provisions, while still others were mounting 10-inch columbiads on the ramparts.

Notwithstanding the praise he gave to Fort Pulaski at the conclusion of his tour, Correspondent Russell was not convinced that Savannah was safe from invasion. He pointed out to General Lawton the weaknesses of the fort. The lowland, he said, made it accessible to boats, and it was open to approach from the rear.

"True enough," Lawton agreed, but added boastfully, "the Commodore will take care of the Yankees at sea and we shall manage them on land!"

Tattnall smiled. "I have no fleet," he said, "and long before the Southern Confederacy has a fleet that can cope with the Stars and Stripes, my bones will be white in the grave."

That night Russell recorded in his diary: "These people all make a mistake in referring to the events of the old war. 'We beat off the British

Blockade of the Savannah River. From *Harper's Pictorial History of the War of 1861.*

fleet at Charleston by the militia—ergo, we'll sink the Yankees now.' They do not understand the nature of the new shells and heavy vertical fire, or the effect of projectiles from great distances falling into works . . . We got back by eight o'clock p. m. after a pleasant day. What I saw did not satisfy me that Pulaski was strong, or Savannah very safe."

On April 9, a private in Company D, 1st Regiment of Georgia, wrote to his mother, "We look for a fight every day. We are well prepared, and the boys are in good spirits 'Spilin' for a fight."

People in the South who were spoiling for a fight did not have long to wait. In Charleston Harbor, at 4:30 on the morning of April 12, 1861, a Confederate mortar at Fort Johnson fired a shell which arched across the sky and burst almost directly over Fort Sumter. With this shot, the tragedy of civil war began.

On May 21, Francis S. Bartow, who had opposed the seizure of Fort Pulaski and yet had served as its first commanding officer under the Georgia flag, led the Oglethorpe Light Infantry to the railroad station to entrain for Virginia. The streets were lined with cheering citizens; the band played "Bold Soldier Boy." Two months later, in a gallant charge on the Federal batteries at Manassas, Bartow, now a brigadier, was shot through the heart.

The Great Expedition

By midsummer, 1861, the North had already planned the strategy that led to the fall of Fort Pulaski. This plan included a naval blockade of the South and the recapture of the southern seacoast fortifications.

On October 29, a combined Army and Navy expedition sailed under sealed orders from Hampton Roads. The great convoy, composed of 51 vessels, moved out to sea in 3 columns—an impressive sight that foreshadowed the amphibious movements of World War II. Twenty-five colliers under gunboat escort had sailed the day before. Army forces numbering more than 12,500 men were under the command of Brig. Gen. Thomas W. Sherman, while the naval squadron and the convoy were commanded by Capt. Samuel F. Du Pont.

At destination, the invading troops were to land in three waves by means of surf boats capable of carrying from 70 to 100 men each. These boats were to approach the beach abreast in line of battle. Infantry, light artillery, and engineers with entrenching tools and sandbags were to go in on the first wave and were expected to overcome initial enemy resistance and dig in on the beach. Heavy field artillery would move in on the second wave and reserves on the third. As soon as the landing had been effected, all boats were to report to the chief quartermaster for unloading supplies.

This plan of battle was never executed, for a few days after sailing the expedition ran into a terrific storm off Cape Hatteras. Several vessels and many of the landing craft were lost. Thus handicapped, General Sherman might have had grave difficulty in securing the beachhead. When the convoy finally reassembled off Port Royal Sound, S. C., the Navy took the initiative. On November 7, Flag Officer

Federal troops land on Hilton Head Island, November 7, 1861. Sketch by W. T. Crane in *The Soldier in Our Civil War.*

Occupation of Tybee Island by Federal troops brings panic to Savannah. Contemporary sketch from *The Soldier in Our Civil War.*

Du Pont led his squadron of steam-propelled vessels to the entrance of the sound where he formed a great oval between the two Confederate forts on Hilton Head and Bay Point. Steaming continuously each vessel fired a broadside as it came opposite one of the forts. So punishing was the effect of this naval bombardment that the Confederates abandoned both fortifications, and the landings on Hilton Head and Bay Point were unopposed. A few days after this initial battle, the town of Port Royal on the mainland fell to the expeditionary force. From these vantage points within sight of Cockspur Island, the Federal troops were made ready to strike at Fort Pulaski.

General Lee Returns to Fort Pulaski

The fall of the forts at Hilton Head and Bay Point and the complete rout of the Confederate forces defending them brought panic to Savannah and the adjacent countryside. It was assumed that the Georgia seaport was the real objective of the Federal expedition, and many people, who could afford it, fled to towns and cities in the interior of the State.

19

At this critical moment Robert E. Lee arrived in Savannah to take charge of the defense. Lee, who had resigned his commission in the United States Army when Virginia seceded from the Union, was now a brigadier general under Confederate colors and had been given command of the forces in South Carolina, Georgia, and east Florida.

The Battle of Port Royal Sound demonstrated to Lee that without adequate naval support it would be impossible to defend the small batteries and forts on the seacoast islands which were all within range of the powerful guns of the Federal fleet. Nor would it be possible to prevent enemy landings on these beach islands without immobilizing thousands of troops for garrison duty, troops that were badly needed in other theaters of war. Even if the manpower could have been spared for island defense, the logistical difficulties of arming and supplying isolated and remote outposts were beyond the capacities of the State or Confederate Governments.

With these considerations in mind, Lee ordered the abandonment of the sea islands of Georgia, the removal of the guns from the batteries, and the withdrawal of the troops to the inner line of defenses on the mainland. This strategy was later confirmed and made the policy of the Confederate Department of War.

On November 10, Tybee Island was abandoned. All batteries were leveled and the heavy guns were ferried across the South Channel to Fort Pulaski. Two companies of infantry from the Tybee garrison were added to the complement at the fort and the remaining troops were withdrawn to Savannah. This was a fateful move for it directly affected the destiny of Fort Pulaski.

At the time, however, no new danger to the fortification on Cockspur Island was anticipated through the abandonment of Tybee Island. It was expected that the fort could defend itself successfully against a naval attack and it was also considered safe from land bombardment. To keep open a line of communications and supply, all side channels leading into the Savannah River above the fort were barred by obstructions. These obstructions, in turn, were protected by floating mines activated by galvanic batteries. The mines, or "infernal machines" as they were called in the naval report, were a new invention which the Confederates borrowed from the Russians. The responsibility for denying the Federal gunboats an opportunity to force a passage through the obstructed side channels into the Savannah River was assigned to Tattnall's flotilla.

In theory, at least, it should have been possible to hold out at Fort Pulaski indefinitely. When the supply line was finally cut, it was not due to any failure in the plan for the protection of the river, but rather to a lack of vigilance on the part of the Georgia Navy, which permitted the Federals to construct strong batteries in the marshes on

Col. Charles H. Olmstead, who defended Fort Pulaski. Courtesy Miss Florence Olmstead.

the north and south banks of the Savannah between the fort and the city.

Twice during November, General Lee inspected the fort on Cockspur Island and gave minute instructions regarding the manner in which it was to be defended. He foresaw the danger of attack from the rear and ordered certain guns to be mounted on the ramparts above the gorge.

Fort Pulaski celebrated Christmas, 1861, in a big way. The men of the garrison felt snug and secure. In the messes, the tables groaned under the weight of delicacies sent down by friends in Savannah. Eggnog parties were held in many of the casemates. Pvt. John Hart of the Irish Jasper Greens wrote exuberantly in his diary: "Fine day here. Plenty of fighting and whisky drinking."

Ten miles away, in the Federal camp on Hilton Head Island, Christmas was not quite so pleasant. The men were kept hard at work digging entrenchments and unloading captured cotton from a steamboat. When the troops were finally released to enjoy themselves, they had to find their own entertainment. Pvt. Charles Lafferty, of the 48th Regiment of New York Volunteers, wrote his sister: "We had a merry Christmas down hear. We bought sassiges of the nigers and hoe cake and build a fir and cooked our sassiages. That is the way we spent our Christmas."

In the summer of 1861, President Lincoln proclaimed a naval block-ade of the South, but it was not until after the Battle of Port Royal Sound, when Flag Officer Du Pont took direct command, that the Union patrols on the Carolina and Georgia coasts became effective. The British Steamer *Fingal,* with munitions, ordnance, and other sup-plies, got through to Savannah on November 13 and had the dis-tinction of being the last ship to run the blockade into that port. Pulaski's share of the cargo was two 24-pounder Blakely rifles and a large number of Enfields. Early in December, Du Pont tightened the stranglehold he already had on the commerce of Savannah by sinking vessels loaded with stone across the channel of the river, and by placing gunboats in Ossabaw and Warsaw Sounds to prevent entrance or escape through these back doors to the port.

After setting up headquarters on Hilton Head Island on the north shore of Tybee Roads, General Sherman kept his men busy repairing and strengthening the fortifications on Port Royal Sound. He con-structed an extensive base for operations and established a hospital. On December 4 he requisitioned siege guns for the proposed attack on Fort Pulaski and not long after he landed a permanent garrison on Tybee Island.

While engaged in these activities Sherman conceived the idea that it might be more advantageous to by-pass Fort Pulaski and make a direct attack on the city of Savannah. He tried to sell this plan to the commander of the naval forces on whom he would have to depend for transport, protection, and assistance in the siege operations he had in mind. Du Pont obligingly ordered a reconnaissance of the winding waterways that led into the Savannah River above Fort Pulaski, but when he discovered how shallow these waterways were at certain stages of the tide, he pronounced the whole scheme im-practical and dangerous. This difference of opinion between the Army and Navy commanders on the conduct of the campaign finally led to the removal of Sherman, but in the meantime the general ordered a tight noose of batteries and gunboats to be thrown around Fort Pulaski.

When the Confederate supply ship, *Ida,* came down the Savannah River on the morning of February 13 on one of her regular trips to the fort, a battery of heavy guns, which the Federals had secretly constructed at Venus Point on the north bank of the river, opened up. The old sidewheeler ran the gauntlet under full steam with shots splashing in her wake. Luck was with her, for the Federal guns, after firing nine shots, recoiled off their platforms. It was the *Ida's* last trip to Pulaski. Two days later she slipped her moorings, ran down the South Channel under the guns of the fort, rounded the point at

Lazaretto, and returned to Savannah through Tybee Creek and the Wilmington Narrows.

During the following week the Federals completed the absolute investment or blockade of Fort Pulaski. They built another strong battery on the south bank of the Savannah River opposite Venus Point and threw a boom across Tybee Creek. To seal this waterway they entrenched two companies of infantry along its bank and assigned a gunboat to patrol the channel. At the same time they destroyed the telegraph line between Savannah and Cockspur Island. From now on neither supplies nor reinforcements could be brought to the fort, nor could the Confederate garrison escape to the mainland. After February 15 the only communication with Savannah was by courier who came and went by night through the marshes, often having to swim the creeks and rivers to avoid the Federal pickets.

Five companies formed the garrison of Fort Pulaski when the fort was cut off. Company B of the Oglethorpe Light Infantry, the German Volunteers, the Washington Volunteers, and the Montgomery Guards were members of the 1st Regiment of Georgia Volunteers. The Macon Wise Guards was accredited to the 25th Regiment of Georgia Regulars. The total strength of the garrison was 385 officers and men. In command was Charles H. Olmstead, who had been elected colonel of the 1st Volunteer Regiment on December 26. To defend the fort there were 48 guns.

The armament was distributed evenly to command all approaches. On the ramparts facing Tybee Island were five 8-inch and four 10-inch columbiads, one 24-pounder Blakely rifle, and two 10-inch seacoast mortars. In the casemates bearing on Tybee were one 8-inch columbiad and four 32-pounder guns, while in batteries outside the fort were two 12-inch and one 10-inch seacoast mortars. The remaining guns were mounted to command the North Channel of the Savannah River and the sweeping marshes to the west.

The New Weapon

The time had come to decide whether to take Fort Pulaski by force or to wait for the garrison to starve. The fort had been provisioned on January 28 with a 6 months' supply of food, which might have been made to last, by careful rationing, to mid-August or even September. Eventually, however, surrender would have been inevitable. Sherman was undoubtedly aware of these circumstances, but he does not seem to have given serious thought to playing a waiting game. The Northern press was clamoring for action, and Sherman, himself, was still bent on the quick capture of Savannah. Whatever merit this dream may have had will never be known, for on February 14 the Commanding

23

Brig. Gen. Q. A. Gillmore, who captured Fort Pulaski.
Harper's Weekly, September 12, 1863. Courtesy Gen. Quincy A.
Gillmore.

General of the United States Army ordered the entire effort of the
expeditionary force to be expended on the reduction of Fort Pulaski.
Long before this order reached headquarters on Hilton Head Island,
Sherman had taken decisive action. On February 19 he sent his Chief
Engineer, Capt. Quincy A. Gillmore, to take command of all troops on
Tybee Island and to prepare for the bombardment of Fort Pulaski.

Gillmore was destined to play the leading role in the Fort Pulask story and win for the fort a permanent niche in the military annals of the United States. A brilliant member of the Corps of Engineers, he is described by the newspaper correspondent, Whitelaw Reid, as "a quick-speaking, quick-moving, soldierly man . . . a fine, wholesome looking, solid six footer, with big head, broad, good humored face, and a high forehead faintly elongated by a suspicion of baldness, curly brown hair and beard, and a frank open face." His greatest attribute as a soldier was a fearless disregard for tradition. At the Battle of Fort Pulaski, Gillmore was breveted a brigadier and later he became a major general of volunteers.

In 1862, Fort Pulaski was considered invincible. Its 7½-foot solid brick walls were backed with massive piers of masonry. The broad waters of the Savannah River and wide swampy marshes surrounded the fort on all sides. Ships of the Navy could not safely come within effective range of this citadel, and there was no firm ground on which land batteries could be erected nearer than Tybee Island, from 1 to 2½ miles away. All previous military experience had taught that beyond a distance of 700 yards smoothbore guns and mortars would have little

Guns were hauled by manpower. From *Harper's Pictorial History of the War of 1861.*

Air view

aski.

chance to break through heavy masonry walls, and beyond 1,000 yards no chance at all.

In referring to Fort Pulaski, the United States Chief of Engineers, General Totten, said "you might as well bombard the Rocky Mountains." General Lee, himself, standing on the parapet of the fort with Colonel Olmstead, pointed to the shore of Tybee Island and remarked, "Colonel, they will make it pretty warm for you here with shells, but they cannot breach your walls at that distance." In the minds of the experts a long-range bombardment would merely serve to pave the way for a direct assault.

Gillmore held a different opinion. He was familiar with the test records of a new weapon, the rifled gun, with which the Army had begun to experiment in 1859, and, on December 1, 1861, he broke with tradition and risked the laughter of his superiors. After a careful reconnaissance he reported to Sherman that it would be possible to reduce Fort Pulaski with mortars and rifled guns from Tybee Island. On this basis he submitted a complete plan for the attack on Fort Pulaski. Sherman approved the plan, but he made it clear that he doubted the usefulness of the rifled guns. In concluding his endorsement he wrote, "All that can be done with guns is to shake the walls in a random manner."

Gillmore Sets the Stage

From the 21st of February, when ordnance and ordnance stores began to arrive in Tybee Roads, until April 9th, Gillmore gave the men of his command no rest. To put his plan for the siege into effect was a Herculean task. Materials, supplies, ammunition, and guns had to be unloaded through the surf and then transported long distances across sand and marsh. Gun emplacements, magazines, bomb-proof shelters, and roads had to be constructed. And last, but not least, gun crews had to be trained.

Detailed to this back-breaking assignment were the 7th Regiment Connecticut Volunteers, the 46th New York Volunteers, two companies of the Volunteer Engineers, and, for most of the time, two companies of the 3rd Rhode Island Volunteer Artillery.

On the northwest shore of Tybee Island facing Fort Pulaski these troops erected 11 batteries for guns and mortars. Their job was made particularly difficult because the last mile of the shore, on which seven of the major batteries had to be established, was an open marsh in full view of the fort and within effective range of its guns. Here all work was performed at night. The men were not allowed to speak above a whisper and were guided by the notes of a whistle. Before dawn each morning evidence of the night's work was concealed by camouflage.

When the batteries were ready, the guns were hauled across the marsh on sling carts. These loads were so extraordinarily heavy that it was often necessary to harness 250 men to a cart. Even on the last night before the bombardment the work continued. In the flickering light of lanterns men filled cartridge bags, cut paper fuses, and whittled wooden fuse plugs.

The final armament comprised 36 pieces placed at various distances from the fort as shown in the following table:

1.	Battery, Stanton,	3 heavy 13-inch Mortars,		at 3,400 yds.
2.	" Grant,	3 " " " "		" 3,200 "
3.	" Lyon,	3 " 10 " Columbiads,		" 3,100 "
4.	" Lincoln,	3 " 8 " "		" 3,045 "
5.	" Burnside,	1 heavy 13 " Mortar,		" 2,750 "
6.	" Sherman,	3 " " " "		" 2,650 "
7.	" Halleck,	2 " " " "		" 2,400 "
8.	" Scott,	{3 10-in.} Columbiads, {1 8-in.}		" 1,740 "
9.	" Sigel,	{5 30-pdr. Parrott, {1 48 " James, (old 24 pdr.)}		" 1,670 "
10.	" McClellan	{2 84 " James, (" 42 ")} {2 64 " James, (" 32 ")}		" 1,650 "
11.	" Totten	2 10-inch Siege Mortars,		" 1,650 "

Eve of Battle

On March 31, when preparations for the bombardment were almost complete, General Sherman was relieved of his command, and responsibility for the campaign in the Department of the South was turned over to Maj. Gen. David Hunter. While this move undoubtedly led to greater harmony of action between Army and Navy leaders, Sherman deserves much of the credit for the successful operations against Pulaski. Neither General Hunter nor Brig. Gen. Henry W. Benham, whom he had placed in command of the Northern District of the Department, suggested a single change in the siege works under construction on Tybee, and Gillmore was retained to conduct the bombardment. On the afternoon of April 9, everything was in readiness to open fire. General orders were issued, the Navy alerted, and the battle set for the following morning.

On Cockspur Island, meanwhile, the Confederates were engaged in making final arrangements to defend Fort Pulaski. The garrison had worked long hours, and the men were weary and apprehensive. In accord with the instructions of General Lee they tore down the

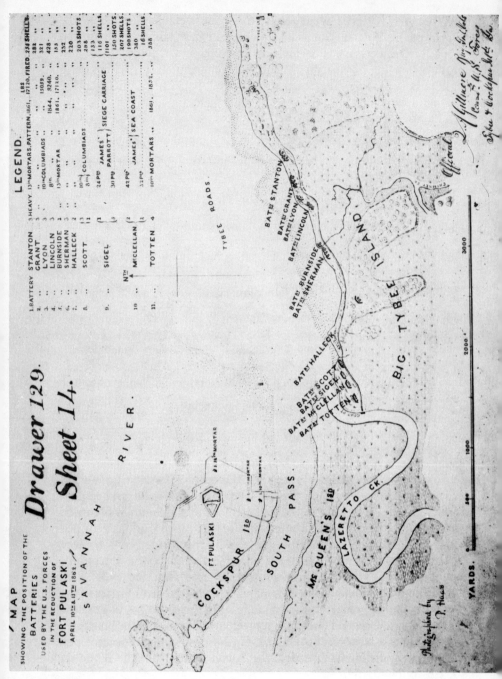

Gillmore's plan for the bombardment. Courtesy National Archives.

Confederates prepar Fort Pulaski for battle. Contemporary drawing made after bombardment for *Harper's Pictorial History of the War of 1861.*

light veranda in front of the officers' quarters and replaced it with a traverse or covered passage made of timbers and earth. They piled sandbags between the guns on the ramparts and dug "rat holes" in the terreplein for the protection of the gunners. To prevent round shot and shell from rolling, they cut the entire parade ground into wide traps and trenches.

In Savannah, on the eve of the battle for Pulaski, a large audience unaware of the impending event, was entertained by Blind Tom, famous Negro pianist, who played his original composition, "The Battle of Manassas."

Bombardment

Morning on the 10th of April 1862, broke clear and cold. A fresh easterly wind whipped the red waters of the Savannah River into whitecaps, and the brown and purple marshes were showing the green of early spring. Soon after sunrise, a lieutenant on duty on the ramparts of Fort Pulaski reported that suspicious changes in the landscape had been made during the night on Tybee Island near the mouth of Tybee Creek. Several old chimneys had been torn down; the top of the ridge had been leveled; brush and trees had been removed; and there were dark objects visible that looked as though they might be guns.

31

While Olmstead and his officers discussed these ominous signs, they saw a small boat put out from the shore of Tybee under a flag of truce and head up the South Channel. Word spread quickly through the fort and men swarmed up to the parapet to watch. Soon the small boat landed at the south wharf. It brought Lt. J. H. Wilson, of the Topographical Engineers, to Cockspur Island with a formal demand to surrender.

Colonel Olmstead retired to his quarters, where, after a brief time, he composed his reply:

> Sir, I have to acknowledge receipt of your communication of this date, demanding the unconditional surrender of Fort Pulaski.
> In reply I can only say, that I am here to defend the Fort, not to surrender it.

Now that the time had come to fight, the men experienced a great sense of relief. They joked and laughed among themselves as they cleaned up the parade ground, carried ammunition to the guns, and prepared for action.

At 10 minutes past 8 o'clock a single 13-inch mortar shell rose from Battery Halleck with a muffled roar. It traveled slowly in a high arc over the fort and exploded in the air beyond. The second mortar shell, from Battery Stanton, fell short, exploding in the marsh east of the fort. And now the line of fire rolled along Tybee Beach, extending itself to right and left as battery after battery unmasked mortars, guns, and columbiads.

For some minutes Pulaski was silent; then, four casemate guns were fired in rapid succession. Almost immediately the guns on the barbette joined in the action directing their fire toward the rifle batteries at King's Landing on Tybee Island.

The first shots on both sides went wide of their marks as the gunners attempted to box their targets. One of the barbette guns of the fort recoiled completely off its chassis, while similar accidents on Tybee put four 10-inch columbiads out of the fight. Despite these early mishaps, the fire from each side was soon rapid and increasingly accurate.

Early in the day the men in the fort learned that they had little to fear from the Federal mortars. Most of the 10-inch and 13-inch mortar shells exploded high in the air or fell outside. The few that dropped on the parade buried themselves in the ground and, on exploding, threw up harmless geysers of mud. Whenever a ponderous solid shot from a columbiad landed squarely on the wall, however, the whole fort quivered and shook. About 2 hours after the fight began, one of these solid shots entered an embrasure and dismounted the casemate gun. Several members of the gun crew were wounded, one so severely that it was necessary to amputate his arm immediately. At 11 o'clock the halyards on the flag pole were cut by a fragment of shell and the flag swooped down within the fort. Lt. Christopher Hussey of the Montgomery Guards and Pvt. John Latham of the German Volunteers sprang upon the parapet and carried the flag under fire to the northeast angle where they raised it again on the ramrod of a cannon.

At noon observers on Tybee counted 47 scars on the south flank, pancoupe, and southeast face of the fort, and it was already obvious that several of the embrasures were considerably enlarged. During the afternoon the fire slackened on both sides, and after sunset not more than 7 or 8 shells an hour were thrown until daylight the next morning. At the end of the day to observers on Tybee, the fort, notwithstanding its dents and scars, looked nearly as solid and capable of resistance as when fire was opened in the morning. There was a general feeling among the Union soldiers that the day's work had not greatly hastened the surrender. The mortars had proved a disappointment and the effect of the breaching fire could not be definitely determined. Although there had been many narrow escapes, no one had been hurt in the Federal batteries.

Had Gillmore been able to inspect the fort at the end of the first day, he would have had reason to rejoice. The place was in shambles. Nearly all of the barbette guns and mortars bearing upon Tybee had been dismounted and only two of the five casemate guns were in order. At the southeast angle, the whole wall from the crest of the parapet to the moat was flaked away to a depth of from 2 to 4 feet.

Surrender

On Friday morning, at daylight, the bombardment reopened with fresh vigor on both sides. Pulaski had repaired some of her guns during the night and now directed her barbette fire with considerable precision and rapidity. From Tybee, Gillmore's gunners resumed the work of breaching with determination, and the effect was almost immediately apparent in the enlargement of the two embrasures on the left of the southeast face of the fort. Pulaski's fire was far less accurate than that of the Federals. The batteries on Tybee were nearly all masked behind a low sand ridge and were also protected by heavy sandbag revetments. Most of the Confederate shot and shell buried themselves in the beach or traveled completely over the Federal batteries and trenches. About 9 o'clock the besiegers received their only casualty. A solid shot from Pulaski entered a gun embrasure in Battery McClellan striking a private soldier and wounded him so severely that he died soon after.

During the morning, the naval gunboat, *Norwich,* began to fire against the northeast face of the fort, but the range was too great and her shots struck only glancing blows on the brick walls. A battery on

Mortar Battery Stanton in action, April 10, 1862. Sketch by
W. T. Crane in Supplement to *Frank Leslie's Illustrated Weekly,*
May 3, 1862.

Long Island opened up at long range from the west, and shots were
landing on the south wall from guns located on a barge in Tybee
Creek.

At noon, a considerable part of the Federal fire was directed against
the guns on the ramparts of the fort and within half an hour these
guns were silenced. By now, two great holes had been opened through
the walls and the inside of the fort was visible from Tybee. The interior
arches had been laid bare, and a barbette gun on the parapet was
tottering, ready to fall. It was plain that the whole east angle would
soon be in ruins. General Benham gave orders to prepare to take
Fort Pulaski by direct assault.

At the fort, when all men were ordered from the ramparts to allow
the guns to cool, Pvt. L. W. Landershine thought that "things looked
blue." One man had been mortally wounded, another had had his
foot taken off by the recoil of a gun, and a dozen others had been
struck by fragments of shell. Projectiles from the rifle batteries were
passing completely through the breach, sweeping across the parade, and
striking against the walls of the north magazine in which 40,000
pounds of black powder was stored.

The moment had come for Olmstead to make a decision. There
were only two courses open. He could fight on against overwhelming
odds, or he could admit defeat. It must have been a difficult choice
for the gallant 25-year-old colonel to make. Impressed by the utter
hopelessness of the situation and believing the lives of the garrison
to be his next care, he gave the order for surrender.

Says Private Landershine, who was at this time discussing the state
of affairs with his comrades, "About 2½ p. m. I seen Col. Olmstead

34

and Capt. Sims go past with a rammer and a sheet, we all knew that it was over with us and we would have to give up."

The Confederate flag was lowered half way and a final gun was fired from a casemate. Then the flag was hauled down and the white sheet took its place. An old era in coastal fortifications had come to an end.

On Tybee there was wild rejoicing. Men danced together on the beach, shook hands, and cheered General Gillmore as he rode along the line. At King's Landing, Gillmore embarked on a small boat with his aides. The passage up the South Channel was rough, the skiff ran aground and was nearly swamped by the heavy seas. Soaked with the salt tides of the Savannah, the party landed at Cockspur Island and advanced toward the fort under a flag of truce. Colonel Olmstead was waiting at the entrance. He showed the way to his quarters, and, during an hour alone with General Gillmore, the terms of the capitulation were settled. After inspecting the fort, the general took leave.

In Colonel Olmstead's quarters by the half-light of candles, the officers of the fort gave up their swords to General Hunter's representative, Maj. Charles G. Halpine. The weapons were laid on a table, and each officer, according to his rank, advanced in turn, mentioned his name and title, and spoke a few words appropriate to the occasion. Said Colonel Olmstead, "I yield my sword, but I trust I have not disgraced it."

The men of the garrison were formed by companies on the parade, stacked their arms, and marched to quarters for the night. The Stars and Stripes was then raised over the ramparts, and Pulaski again became part of the possessions, as well as the property, of the Union.

Terms of the surrender were unconditional.

Significance of the Siege

In its relation to the total strategy of the Civil War, the reduction of Fort Pulaski was important. The blockade directed against the South was materially strengthened by the acquisition of this fortress in the mouth of the Savannah River. After the surrender, Northern troops occupied the fort and commanded the entrance to the principal port of Georgia. It thus served as one of the many pincers that throttled the economic life of the South.

When viewed in larger perspective, however, an even greater significance may be attached to the battle for the once-great fort. "The result of this bombardment," General Hunter declared in his report to the Secretary of War, "must cause a change in the construction of fortifications as radical as that foreshadowed in naval architecture by the conflict between the *Monitor* and *Merrimac*. No works of stone or brick can resist the impact of rifled artillery of heavy calibre." Subsequent events verified this prophetic statement, and the Fort Pulaski incident may be considered one of the many mileposts in history. The strategy that had guided military experts had to be revised to meet the threat of a new weapon of war, and Fort Pulaski, because of the consequent changes, has become an interesting relic of another age.

In the 2 days of battle, 5,275 shot and shell were fired against the fort, but the breach through the walls was largely the result of three guns—two 84-pounder and one 64-pounder James rifles. Solid projectiles from these guns at a distance of 1,640 yards penetrated the brickwork from 20 to 25 inches with shattering lateral effect. Shots from the other rifles were erratic in flight—some wabbling, some turning end-over-end—and did little damage when they slammed into the wall of the fort. Explosive shells from the rifles also played an important part in reducing the work.

The guns and mortars in the Federal batteries were served by detachments from the 7th Connecticut Volunteers, the 3rd Rhode Island Volunteer Artillery, the 46th New York State Volunteers, and the 8th Maine Volunteers. On the second day of the bombardment 100 sailors from the frigate *Wabash* manned four of the 30-pounder Parrott rifles in Battery Sigel. The accuracy of fire achieved by the gunners in the 2-day battle is remarkable in view of the fact that none of them, except the sailors, had had previous experience in firing.

The quick reduction of Fort Pulaski took the world by surprise, and, until the details of the battle were available, many people regarded the surrender with suspicion. In the circumstances, however, Olmstead's decision was wise. Nothing but glory could have been obtained by prolonging the battle, and many additional lives might have been lost. When the Confederates gave up Tybee Island, they abandoned Pulaski to its fate, for they presented the Union forces with the only possible battery sites from which the fort could have been reduced. When Olmstead raised the white flag, the Federals were already preparing an assault, and within 24 hours they could have thrown more than 10,000 troops against the fort. Opposed by such odds, the handful of men on Cockspur, no matter how brave they might have been, could have staged but a brief and pointless resistance.

Pulaski's captured garrison was sent North to Governor's Island in New York Harbor, where the officers were confined in Fort Columbus; the men, in Castle Williams. Three months later the officers were transferred to Johnson's Island near Sandusky, Ohio, and the men, to Fort Delaware. Many of the prisoners died of pneumonia or typhoid fever and a considerable number of the privates, because of family connections in the Northern States or lack of sympathy with the Confederate cause, took the oath of allegiance to the United States. In

August, most of the men were exchanged at Aiken's Landing on the James River, 12 miles from Richmond, Va., and were soon back in Savannah. The officers were exchanged in September at Vicksburg, Miss.

The honor of being the first Federal troops to garrison Fort Pulaski after the surrender was given to the 7th Connecticut Regiment, one company of the 3rd Rhode Island Heavy Artillery, and a detachment of the Volunteer Engineers. On June 1 the 7th Connecticut was relieved by the 48th New York, which remained on Cockspur until May 31, 1863. The so-called honor of garrison duty was tempered with hard work, for, during the months following the battle, the troops were detailed to repair the damage caused by the bombardment. The batteries on Tybee Island were dismantled and some of the guns were added to the armament of the fort. To ease the tedium of life on a small island, the 48th New York organized a baseball team, a band, and a dramatic association, and the wives of some of the officers came to live on Cockspur.

The war continued actively on other fronts, slowly turning against the South. Weeks, months, and years passed. In June 1863 Pulaski's garrison was reduced to a holding force. Great battles were fought

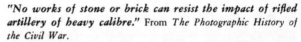

"No works of stone or brick can resist the impact of rifled artillery of heavy calibre." From *The Photographic History of the Civil War.*

elsewhere—Vicksburg, Gettysburg, Chickamauga, Chattanooga, Lookout Mountain, Missionary Ridge, the Wilderness, Spotsylvania, and Kennesaw Mountain. In September 1864, Gen. William Tecumseh Sherman took Atlanta after a long and bloody siege and prepared to march to Savannah through the breadbasket of the Confederate States.

"The Immortal Six Hundred"

Late in October 1864, Fort Pulaski became involved in one of the most barbaric episodes of the Civil War when more than 500 prisoners of war—Confederate officers of rank from lieutenant to lieutenant colonel—were brought to Cockspur from a stockade on Morris Island in Charleston Harbor. These officers, captured in battle and representing every Southern State and the border States of Missouri, Maryland, and Kentucky, were the victims of a cruel policy of retaliation and are known in Southern history as "The Immortal Six Hundred."

The dismal story began at Charleston when Confederate Gen. Samuel Jones, in an attempt to lift the bombardment of that city, adopted a dangerous stratagem of using prisoners of war as a shield. On June 13, 1864, Jones notified Union Gen. J. G. Foster, Commandant of the Department of the South, that 5 generals and 45 field officers of the U. S. Army had been quartered in a part of the city which for many months had been exposed night and day to the fire of Federal guns. Foster immediately retaliated by requesting that 55 Confederate Officers of equal rank be sent from the prison at Fort Delaware to be placed in a stockade on Morris Island under the guns of Fort Sumter.

This ugly situation was ended by a general exchange of the officers on August 3, but on that day Jones placed 600 more Federal officers in the residential section of Charleston, which was under bombardment. Federal reaction was prompt. Six hundred additional Confederate officers were sent down from Fort Delaware and this time they were placed in the stockade on Morris Island under the guns of Fort Sumter.

What benefit Jones really expected to derive from his strategy is certainly not clear. There is evidence that he soon regretted the game he was playing and made every effort possible to have the Federal officers moved out of Charleston, but, due to the fortunes of war, Jones was powerless to stop the chain of events he had started. He could not get rid of his unwelcome guests, and, as General Sherman, poised for his march through Georgia, threatened the security of the Confederate prison at Andersonville, Ga., hundreds of new Federal prisoners sent from that place began to arrive in Charleston every day.

In October, Fate intervened. Yellow fever, which had been smoldering in Charleston for many weeks, became epidemic, and the acute

38

Third Rhode Island Artillery at Fort Pulaski. From *The Photographic History of the Civil War.*

danger from this source gave Jones the excuse to remove the prisoners without authority from his superiors. He sent the officers to Columbia and the men to Florence. On learning of this move, Foster ordered the Confederate prisoners from Morris Island to Fort Pulaski.

When the "Immortal Six Hundred" arrived at Cockspur Island, they presented a forlorn picture. Uniforms in tatters, barefooted, suffering from diarrhea and hacking coughs, their ranks had already been reduced to 520. Forty-nine were in hospitals, 4 had escaped, 2 had been exchanged, and 2 had taken the oath of allegiance. Six were in a convict prison on Hilton Head Island for attempted escape, 13 were unaccounted for, and 4 were buried in the sands of Morris Island.

Review of the 48th New York Volunteers on Fort Pulaski parade ground. From *History of the 48th Regiment New York Volunteers in the War for the Union, 1861–1865.*

At Fort Pulaski, Col. Philip P. Brown, Jr., commandant of the post, greeted the prisoners and promised to make the fort the model military prison of the United States. He said that he had already requisitioned blankets and clothing, full army rations, and plenty of fuel.

Colonel Brown, 157th New York Volunteers, was a completely humane man and won the respect of his Confederate prisoners, but he could not carry out the promises he had made. His requisitions were ignored. In consequence, he could issue neither blankets nor clothing. Out of his garrison supplies he fed the prisoners as well as he could, but fuel on Cockspur was scarce and fires in the cookstoves could be lighted but once a day. When the weather turned cold there was neither wood nor coal to heat the prison casemates. Because of his attitude of humanity, Brown drew upon himself the censure of his commanding general.

On December 15, Brown was ordered to impose a starvation ration composed of one-quarter pound of bread, 10 ounces of cornmeal, and one-half pint of pickles daily, and 1 ounce of salt every 5 days. Under this new order prisoners were permitted to secure additional food from sutlers, but since they had no money and were not allowed to receive funds from the Confederate States, they could purchase no food.

For 43 days in the coldest months of an unusually severe winter, the prisoners at Pulaski subsisted on this cornmeal and pickle diet. Cats and dogs that strayed through the prison bars were immediately cooked and eaten. But day by day the men grew weaker. At night, with no blankets and no warming fires, they had to keep moving about or freeze. By mid-January 1865, scurvy began to take its toll.

Meanwhile, Savannah had surrendered to General Sherman, and as a result the Federal forces in the far South were entirely reorganized. On January 21, Fort Pulaski became a part of the District of Savannah under the command of Bvt. Maj. Gen. Cuvier Grover, U. S. Volunteers, and, on January 27, following an inspection by Grover's medical director, Pulaski's prisoners were put back on full rations. This timely action saved the lives of many of the men. On March 5 the long ordeal was ended. Four hundred and sixty-five survivors of the original "Six Hundred" were returned to Fort Delaware.

The Last Salute

Now the actors come on stage for the final curtain in the drama of Fort Pulaski! Sherman had rested in Savannah and had gone north through the Carolinas to Bentonville and Durham. Grant had met Lee at Appomattox. The defenders of Fort Sumter had laid down their arms. The Confederate armies had been crushed on the battlefields. Gillmore had returned to command the Department of the South, and the destiny of Fort Pulaski was again in his hands.

Prisoners' newspaper, Fort Pulaski, March 2, 1865. Courtesy
Mrs. Irving McKesson.

On April 29, 1865, 200 guns were fired from the ramparts of Fort
Pulaski to mark the surrender of General Lee—the end of a great
military career which had begun on Cockspur Island more than 35
years before.

A few weeks later the conquering forces captured the President of
the Confederate States. In command of the detail which took Mr.
Davis was Brig. Gen. J. H. Wilson, of the Topographical Engineers,
who 3 years before had brought to Fort Pulaski the demand for surrender. Mr. Davis was captured in middle Georgia and sent down
the Savannah River to Hilton Head Island for transport to Fortress
Monroe. Accused of complicity in the assassination of Abraham Lincoln and under orders to be treated as a dangerous criminal, the
Confederate president spent his last night in Georgia aboard ship in
the lee of Cockspur Island. Next morning as he was brought to Hilton
Head, Negroes, lining the shores of the islands, chanted "We'll hang
Jeff Davis to the sour apple tree!"

To the grim fort on Cockspur Island were brought leaders of the
Confederacy, some to remain many months in prison, while an angry
nation sought the illusive satisfaction of vengeance. In the list of dis-
tinguished prisoners were 3 cabinet officers: Secretary of State Robert
M. T. Hunter, Secretary of the Treasury George A. Trenholm, and
Secretary of War James A. Seddon, as well as Assistant Secretary of

41

War John A. Campbell. In addition, there were 3 State governors, Andrew G. Magrath of South Carolina, Andrew B. Moore of Alabama, and Alexander K. Allison of Florida; 1 senator, David L. Yulee of Florida; and Brig. Gen. Hugh W. Mercer, who as colonel of the 1st Regiment of Georgia had once been in command of Fort Pulaski.

The Confederacy had been defeated and the streets of Savannah were patrolled by blue-clad soldiers, but the spirit of the men and women, who more than 4 years before had demanded the seizure of Fort Pulaski, was still unbroken. The stores were all open. Business of every sort progressed precisely as usual. The streets were filled with native citizens, dressed somewhat antiquely, but giving no sign of suffering. A smart sailor from a Federal gunboat summed up the scene, "Hell," he said, "this town isn't dead; it's wound up and running." "It was the rebel Savannah unchanged," wrote Whitelaw Reid, the famous war correspondent.

Cockspur Island After 1865

With the return of peace, the Corps of Engineers under the direction of General Gillmore undertook to modernize and strengthen Fort Pulaski. Between the years 1869 and 1872, they remodeled the demilune, constructing underground magazines and passageways and emplacements for heavy guns. Major changes were also planned for the main fortification, but, after digging a huge excavation in the north end of the parade ground and laying massive concrete piers, the job was abandoned. Proposals were already under consideration for a new coast artillery post on Tybee Island, which would take the place of Fort Pulaski.

After 1872 no further active military use of the fort was ever made, except briefly during the Spanish-American War when a small force was garrisoned there to man the guns that had been installed in the demilune and at Battery Horace Hambright, on the north shore of the island, and to operate the controls for electric mines in the mouth of the Savannah River. For many years the only inhabitants of the fort were an ordnance sergeant and a lightkeeper. After the great hurricane of 1891, when the sea rose 5 feet over the parade ground, a 2-story house for the lightkeeper was erected on the top of the fort.

In the first years of the 20th century, Fort Pulaski and the eastern part of Cockspur Island were totally abandoned. The moat around the fort and demilune filled with mud from the river; the tides swept over the neglected dikes and flooded the low-lying marshes. The parade ground became a veritable jungle and hundreds of snakes made their homes in the innumerable crevices in the fort's masonry. Infrequent parties of zealous hunters and hardy pilgrims, willing to wade through the soft marsh, were the only visitors.

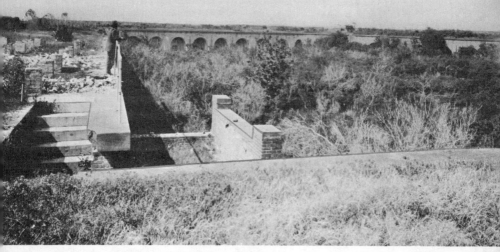

Abandoned and desolate. Photo by Geoffrey King, 1925.

Decontamination facilities to receive German prisoners of war were prepared in 1918 at the U. S. Quarantine Station on the west end of Cockspur Island, but the war ended before this installation was put to use.

Meanwhile, the War Department took the first step toward the preservation of Fort Pulaski, announcing on July 17, 1915, that this fortification had been selected to be a national monument under the American Antiquities Act. Further action was delayed by World War I. In 1918, Col. John Millis, District Engineer at Savannah, visited Fort Pulaski and was so impressed by the magnificence of the ruin that he recommended immediate preservation. The next district engineer, Col. F. W. Alstaetter, was equally interested in the project, and, largely through his efforts, the Savannah Board of Trade and other organizations began to seek national monument status for the fort. On January 7, 1924, Representative Charles G. Edwards, 1st District of Georgia, introduced a bill in Congress to bring about this desired result. The efforts of these individuals and organizations were rewarded on October 15, 1924, when Fort Pulaski was made a national monument by proclamation of President Calvin Coolidge.

The fort remained in desolate condition, however, until 1933 when the national monument was transferred by the War Department to the Department of the Interior, and the National Park Service began the development of the area.

The plan adopted in the restoration of Fort Pulaski was not to reproduce any one definite period in the history of the fortification, but rather to protect the structure from further deterioration by making

43

Fort Pulaski during and after restoration by the National Park Service.

The Moat.

The parapet.

The quarters.

The sally port.

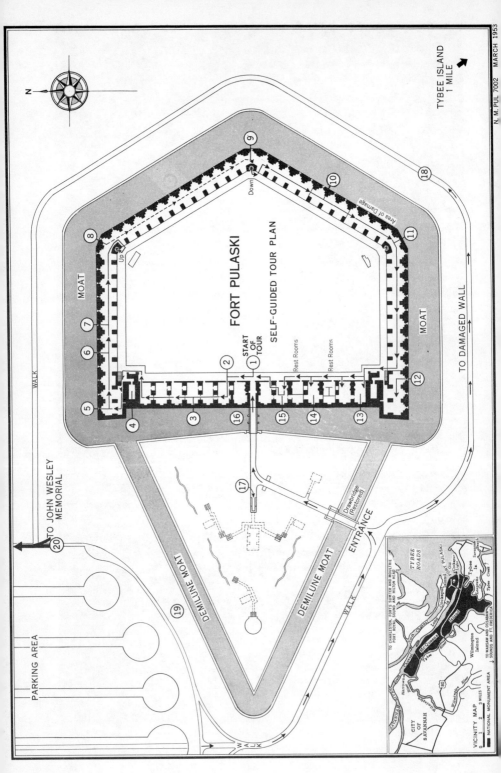

FORT PULASKI

SELF-GUIDED TOUR PLAN

48

essential repairs and to restore only where necessary to illustrate the use and history of certain features of the fort.

Original plans and specifications were available in the files of the War Department for practically all of the items of restoration and repair work undertaken. The restoration of the fort and the development of the national monument were accomplished with funds provided by the Public Works Administration and through the labor of the Civilian Conservation Corps. In 1938, Cockspur Island was joined to McQueens Island by the construction of a bridge across the South Channel of the Savannah River. From 1942 to 1947 the fort was closed to the public, when Cockspur Island, as the site of a Navy Section Base, again became an active part of the defense system of the United States.

Fort Pulaski is a large-scale outdoor exhibit. The main structure, together with outlying works, including demilune, drawbridges, ditches, and dikes, is a fine example of past military architecture. As a vivid reminder of past events it presents an important phase of our great national heritage.

Guide to the Area

Fort Pulaski, resembling a medieval castle, is surrounded by a wide moat, with two drawbridges, and a rear fortification known as a demilune. After crossing the outer drawbridge, a short walk through the demilune will bring you to the second drawbridge and the sally port or only entrance into the main fortification.

Numbered markers have been placed at significant points of interest. These markers correspond with the numbers of the text below and with those shown on the guide map. They should be followed in consecutive order.

1. THE SALLY PORT. The fort entrance is equipped with many devices for last-ditch defense. The massive drawbridge, weighing several tons, is raised by winches and counterweights which may be seen in the rooms on either side of the entrance. As the drawbridge rises, a strong wooden grill, called the portcullis, drops through a slot in the granite lintel overhead. The heart-pine doors are studded with iron bolts to make it difficult to chop through them with axes. Within the sally port are two recesses for the protection of guards and 10 slits, or loopholes, through the side walls for small arms fire. In time of great danger, the inner doors could also be shut and barred.

2. THE GORGE. The western, or rear, section of Fort Pulaski is known as the gorge ("throat") because it contains the sally port, or entrance of the fort. The living quarters are also in the gorge. Enlisted men

Bronze howitzer in northwest bastion.

Arched gun galleries.

occupied the barracks rooms, or casemates, to the north of the entrance; officers were quartered in the casemates to the south of the entrance. The word casemate means a bomb-proof shelter. Each of the arched chambers surrounding the parade ground is a casemate. During the Civil War, when a large number of troops was stationed at Fort Pulaski, most of the enlisted men were quartered in the casemated gun galleries or in tents. Originally, all of the casemates were closed in with wooden fronts to provide shelter from rain and cold. The parade ground, on which the men exercised and drilled, is 2½ acres in extent. The covered veranda, which runs the length of the gorge, is an unusual feature in fort architecture.

3. BARRACKS ROOMS. When Georgia troops seized Fort Pulaski in 1861, the barracks rooms were unfurnished. The Confederates built triple-decker bunks against the walls and filled mattress covers with hay from the parade ground. They brought chairs, tables, and camp cots from their homes in Savannah. After the surrender, Federal troops added many items of furniture obtained by raiding plantations along the coast. The rooms were lighted by candles, coal-oil lanterns, and lamps. The large fireplace in each room was equipped with a crane and other devices for cooking, but both Confederate and Union soldiers did most of their cooking on field ranges. While walking through the barracks rooms, note how the loopholes in the rear wall are variously angled to give a wide range of fire.

4. THE NORTH MAGAZINE. On the second day of the bombardment Federal projectiles, exploding near the entrance to this powder magazine, threatened to blow up the Confederates with their own powder. The interior walls of the magazine are from 12 to 15 feet thick.

5. THE NORTHWEST BASTION. A bastion is a part of a fort which extends out from the main wall, with embrasures and loopholes to permit lateral fire along the walls. Fort Pulaski had only demibastions, or half bastions, as they extend out only in one direction and give protection to only one wall. The rectangular openings through the outer walls of the fort are embrasures to permit the firing of cannon. The embrasures in the bastions are angled to bring a crossfire on the main drawbridge and on the point of the demilune. The slot under each embrasure was to receive the tongue of a gun carriage which was then held in place by a large iron pin dropped through the round hole in the floor of the embrasure. The openings in the ceiling above the embrasures are smoke vents. The circular grooves in the floor originally held iron tracks on which the wheels of the gun carriages turned. The slots and grilled trapdoors in the floors of the casemates are to provide ventilation under the floors. The round pegs in the floor cover iron spikes that hold the planks in place and originally served to

reduce the hazard of a powder explosion when the guns were in use. Hobnails in soldiers' boots on contact with exposed spikes might have resulted in a dangerous shower of sparks.

6. THE GUN GALLERIES.　The casemated gun galleries, which surround the parade ground on four sides and give to Fort Pulaski the atmosphere of a cloistered monastery, contain fine examples of brick masonry. The arches were constructed over wooden forms, each brick being hand cut to fit its special place. The joints were mortared from above and, when the arches were firm and strong, the wooden forms were removed.

7. THE WATER SYSTEM.　Under the brick pavements, which replace the wooden floors in the two center casemates of each gallery, are water cisterns. There are 10 of these cisterns, or storage tanks, in the fort, each capable of holding 20,000 gallons of water. During rainstorms, water falling on the top of the fort seeps through about 3 feet of earth and a foot of oyster shell until it reaches the lead-covered brick roof, whence it is diverted through pipes to the cisterns. Overflow water from the roof emerges through weep holes between the arches high on the walls facing the parade ground.

The damaged wall.

8. THE TERREPLEIN. The flat surface on top of the rampart of the fort is called the terreplein and contains brick and granite platforms for mounting guns. From this high level, guns had a range of fire greater than those mounted in the casemates below. The breast-high parapet on the outer edge of the terreplein was for the protection of both guns and gun crews. The recesses in the parapet wall were to allow gun carriages to swing freely.

9. TERREPLEIN, EAST ANGLE. From this point a good view may be obtained of the shore of Tybee Island, from which the fort was bombarded. The two batteries containing the 10 James and Parrott rifled guns, which did the principal damage to the fort, were located on the western point of Tybee just north of the present highway bridge. The 9 other batteries of mortars and siege guns were at various places along the shore for 2 miles in the direction of the lighthouse. The small brick lighthouse on Cockspur Point was built about 1840 and therefore was a feature of the landscape at the time of the bombardment.

10. THE PRISON. From October 23, 1864, to March 4, 1865, the northeast, southeast, and part of the south casemates of Fort Pulaski were used as a military prison.

11. THE BREACH. In three casemates at the southeast angle there are solid brick walls without embrasures. These walls were constructed in 1862, after the surrender, by troops of the 48th New York Volunteers to close the breach, or opening, made by the Federal shot and shell during the bombardment.

12. THE SOUTHWEST BASTION. The interior of the southwest bastion was destroyed by fire in 1893. This part of the fort has been left unrestored to show details of the foundation construction. All arches are completed beneath the floor level and are laid on a platform of yellow pine timbers, called grillage. The grillage in turn is supported by yellow pine piles which are driven deep into the mud of Cockspur Island.

13. HEADQUARTERS (SURRENDER ROOM). The surrender of Fort Pulaski was executed in the quarters of Col. Charles H. Olmstead, Confederate commander. In 1925 a lightning fire destroyed the officers' quarters. This room was restored in 1935.

14. CISTERN ROOM. This room, also destroyed in the 1925 fire, has been left unrestored to show construction details. The cylindrical brick structure below floor level is the top of a water cistern.

15. BOTTLE COLLECTION. Nearly 1,000 bottles were found in the Fort Pulaski moat when the mud was cleaned out in 1935. These bottles had been thrown into the moat by workmen building the fort and by Confederate and Union soldiers during the Civil War. A part of the collection is shown in this room.

16. THE MOAT. The wet ditch, or moat, which completely surrounds the main fortification and the demilune, varies in width from 30 to 48 feet. It has an average depth of 7 feet. The water, brought through a canal from the South Channel of the Savannah River, is controlled through a series of tide gates. Fish, crabs, shrimp, oysters, and turtles live in the moat.

17. THE DEMILUNE. The outwork often found at the rear of a large fortification was originally constructed in a half-moon shape—hence the name demilune. The principal earthworks in the demilune were built in 1869, after the Civil War, and contain four powder magazines and passageways connecting gun emplacements. The detached mound of earth near the entrance to the demilune was erected in 1893 to protect an underground chamber in which were placed the controls for electric mines in the main channel of the Savannah River. This room is kept locked today as it contains a large and dangerous electric transformer.

18. DAMAGED WALL. Evidence of the bombardment can best be seen from the outside of the fort. The breach through the southeast angle was repaired in 1862 with a bright-red brick, which, in contrast to the original brown brick, shows the area of the damage wrought by the siege guns. The southeastern wall facing Tybee is pock-marked by shell hits, and many of the balls and projectiles are still embedded in the brickwork.

19. THE CEMETERY. On the glacis, or north bank of the demilune moat, a small cemetery was established when the fort was under construction. Here, during the Civil War, both Confederate and Union soldiers were temporarily buried. The 8-inch columbiad, which marks the site, was a Confederate gun damaged in the bombardment.

20. THE WAVING GIRL. Just after the Civil War a girl was born on Cockspur Island in the former quarters of the engineer officers. The child was named Florence Martus, and her father was an ordnance sergeant at Fort Pulaski. From the stone pier on the north shore of Cockspur Island young Florence first saw the passing ships going with cargoes to the farthest corners of the earth. The small child was fascinated by these gay ships and waved her handkerchief. Sailors on the ships waved back. A few years later, the child, then in her 'teens,

John Wesley Memorial erected in 1951 by the Georgia Society, Colonial Dames of America, to commemorate the landing of Wesley on Cockspur Island, February 6, 1736.

went to live with her brother, a light keeper, in a white cottage close by the riverbank, about 5 miles up river from Fort Pulaski. From this time on she waved at every ship that passed—a table cloth or towel by day, a lantern by night. For more than 44 years she never missed a ship, and each ship, as it passed, returned her salute with three blasts of the whistle. Many stories were told of this small girl, who finally grew to be a white-haired old lady. These legends of the Waving Girl of Savannah are known in all the seas where ships have sailed.

How to Reach the Monument

Fort Pulaski, on Cockspur Island at the mouth of the Savannah River, is 15 miles east of Savannah, Ga., and may be reached from that city by way of U. S. 80 (Tybee Highway). The entrance to the monument is on McQueens Island at U. S. 80. Cockspur Island is connected by a short road and a concrete bridge across the South Channel of the Savannah River.

Administration

Fort Pulaski National Monument is administered by the National Park Service of the United States Department of the Interior. Communications should be addressed to the Superintendent, Fort Pulaski National Monument, Box 204, Savannah Beach, Ga.

About Your Visit

You may visit Fort Pulaski daily, except Christmas, from 8:30 a. m. to 5:30 p. m. Information may be obtained from attendants on duty inside the fort, and brief lectures are given at frequent intervals by the historian. A nominal admission charge is made at the fort entrance. Children under 12 years of age are admitted free when accompanied by adults assuming responsibility for their safety and orderly conduct. Organized groups of school children between the ages of 12 and 18 are also admitted free.

Related Areas

Other seacoast fortifications in the National Park System are: Castle Clinton National Monument, in New York Harbor; Fort McHenry National Monument and Historic Shrine, at Baltimore, Md.; Fort Sumter National Monument, in Charleston Harbor, S. C.; Fort Frederica National Monument, Ga.; Castillo de San Marcos and Fort Matanzas National Monuments, at St. Augustine, Fla.; Fort Jefferson National Monument, in the Dry Tortugas Islands, about 68 miles from Key West, Fla.; and San Juan National Historic Site, San Juan, Puerto Rico.

U.S. GOVERNMENT PRINTING OFFICE : 1961 O—586735

U. S. 80 through Fort Pulaski National Monument.

DATE DUE

SE 12'89			